Contents

Introduction

Many sales professionals associate the term "process" with rigid scripts and reports created by individuals unfamiliar with the challenges of meeting sales quotas. Some claim to have a sales process but struggle to articulate its specifics. In contrast, successful salespeople can precisely outline their actions before, during, and after each sales call. This book will comprehensively address the why, what, and how of a highly effective sales process, offering insights to integrate it seamlessly into your routine. You will learn to compete at a global level, cultivating loyal clients who consistently seek your assistance.

The sales landscape is undergoing significant changes with globalization, technological advancements, and increased competition. Customers now control the sales cycle, researching and deciding on purchases independently. Four key shifts impact sales: 1) Customers initiate the buying cycle independently, often online. 2) Customers seek a personalized experience and value beyond products or services. 3) Collaboration with other departments, like marketing and customer service, is essential. 4) The marketplace is diverse, requiring an understanding of various customer segments. Success in today's sales landscape demands adaptability and a comprehensive understanding of the evolving marketplace and consumer dynamics.

In the TV show "24," Jack Bauer's aggressive interrogation style inspired some salespeople to adopt a similarly intense approach when asking sales questions. There is fine line between effective questioning and an intrusive interrogation. By understanding the customer's perspective and framing questions within a larger business conversation, you can create a connection, enhance credibility, increase urgency, and clarify value. This approach transforms the questioning process into a beneficial conversation for the prospect, fostering information gathering, urgency, and lasting relationships.

Ever been overwhelmed by data and analytics during a presentation? We'll explore the potency of combining storytelling with data, delving into why this combination is highly effective and taps into our primal instincts. We'll address problem-solving through storytelling and provide frameworks to seamlessly integrate analytics into your narrative. Learn to distill your data story to its core and enhance your skills as an analytics storyteller, ultimately transforming how you communicate with data.

You've navigated the sales process diligently, confident in the value of your offering. Post-presentation, instead of a positive response, the buyer expresses hesitancy due to objections. Effectively handling objections distinguishes successful sales professionals from others. Overcoming objections is challenging, requiring thorough preparation. While there's no one-size-fits-all solution, key suggestions include understanding the buyer-salesperson relationship, anticipating potential obstacles, asking probing questions to uncover real issues, and confidently addressing common objections. Ready to explore strategies for overcoming objections?

Negotiation skills have been taught for decades, but recent changes, including increased buyer information from the internet, widespread familiarity with negotiation skills due to reality TV, and a better understanding of brain reactions during negotiations, have altered the landscape. We'll focus on enhancing your negotiation abilities, emphasizing the distinct skills required in sales. You'll explore why compromise is not effective and learn how to create enduring deals. The goal is to make you a more successful and enjoyable negotiator.

You've successfully generated a lead, turning it into a promising opportunity for a significant sale. Your updates have caught the attention of your manager and colleagues, creating a mix of excitement and pressure. After a successful presentation and addressing buyer concerns, you've reached a crucial point that distinguishes top sales professionals. It's time to confidently ask for the business and close the sale. This stage can be challenging, requiring full confidence and preparation. While there's no one-size-fits-all approach, I have suggestions to consider as you craft your closing strategy.

Salespeople face immense hustle and bustle, but now they have powerful allies in AI and automation tools. These tools aren't just beneficial for salespeople; they also bring advantages to companies. By automating tasks, reducing human errors, and handling vast data efficiently, these tools offer clear benefits. I'll guide you through the complex and evolving landscape. We'll explore where these advantages lie and how they can help you save time, alleviate stress, and enhance relationships with both customers and superiors.

Chapter 1 Managing Your Sales Process

Why a sales process is key

Life is filled with routines, or processes, that we often take for granted. These are essentially habits we've developed, like the routine we follow when coming home from work. In sales, where numerous tasks demand attention, having a structured sales process is crucial. It enhances efficiency, organizes company roles, boosts revenue, and improves forecasting accuracy. Some may find the idea uncomfortable, but a well-established sales process is key to a salesperson's success, providing consistency, clarity, and continuous improvement. Embracing a sales process as a habit ensures better results and impactful customer interactions.

What is a sales process?

A sales process is a series of defined stages and repeatable steps guiding salespeople from lead to customer. Think of it as a map for a mountain climb, helping navigate from the base to the summit. Stages, activities, and verifiable outcomes are essential components. Common steps include prospecting, contact, qualification, needs assessment, presentation, proposal, handling objections, gaining commitment, and follow-up. A customer-focused process eliminates unproductive actions, adding momentum toward commitment. A good sales process is flexible, scalable, and aligns with CRM systems for effective tracking and progression. Understanding these elements ensures a successful climb up the sales mountain.

Steps of a typical sales process

A well-defined sales process is more than just closing a deal; it guides the customer's journey from prospecting to post-purchase. It fosters lasting relationships, increasing customer lifetime value and reducing acquisition costs. The key steps include prospecting, making a good first impression, qualifying leads, conducting effective customer conversations, seamless onboarding, and post-purchase follow-up. Customizing these steps to fit your business needs ensures a successful sales process, acting as a map to guide prospects from initiation to the sales summit.

What is a sales methodology?

Your sales process is the map guiding prospects from start to finish, while your sales methodology provides the skills and techniques for effective navigation. Both are crucial, working in tandem for maximum impact. Sales methodologies, like the topology on a map, help navigate through stages with intentionality.

They empower salespeople with proven approaches based on buying principles and field-tested tactics. For instance, an inbound sales methodology attracts prospects, and customer conversation methodology guides the story from opening to commitment. These methodologies are actionable how-to guides aligning with prospect and buyer needs throughout the sales cycle. Effective implementation requires organization-wide adoption, efficient training, and scalable coaching to build and refine sales skills. In essence, having a great map is essential, but being a skilled navigator at each stage is equally crucial for reaching the sales summit consistently.

How to leverage your methodology

In my view, the most crucial part of any sales methodology is the approach used in customer conversations. Your mindset matters; a service-oriented approach trumps a selling mindset. In the neuro selling customer conversation model, start by establishing a genuine connection and building personal trust. Share a personal connection story to set a positive tone. Then, introduce the prospect story to demonstrate understanding of their goals. Present the problem story, using third-party insights to highlight obstacles hindering the prospect's goals. Quantify the cost of not solving these problems. Transition to your product or solution story, showcasing differentiation and aligning your solution with previously discussed problems. Compare the solution's price to the problem's cost to illustrate real value. Identify and remove barriers to change, leading to a commitment. Mastering this methodology yields immediate benefits in sales and customer satisfaction.

Understand your buyer

Often, organizations design their sales process without considering the buyer's perspective, focusing too much on showcasing their company's features. It's crucial to develop a sales process with the buyer in mind, aligning it with their journey and needs. Just as car manufacturers tailor features to consumer demands, your sales process should adapt to what buyers seek. Understanding the buyer's journey, including pre-call planning, social media presence, and providing useful information during prospecting, is essential. Recognizing that buyers may not initially realize they need your product is part of effective prospecting. The evaluation stage requires establishing a connection, sharing insights, and demonstrating how your solution addresses their needs. The sales process extends beyond the sale, addressing buyer concerns and encouraging referrals. By focusing on the buyer's journey, your sales process becomes more natural, leading to increased sales and buyer satisfaction.

Document your sales process

While having a great sales process is beneficial, documenting it is crucial for accountability and efficiency. Follow these five key steps to effectively document your process:

1. Define the buying process from the buyer's perspective, outlining their steps from problem recognition to contract execution.

2. Fill in supporting details by putting yourself in the prospect's shoes and answering key questions at each stage.

3. Identify actions at each stage to help the prospect move forward based on their needs.

4. Determine how to measure progress, creating reporting requirements for the organization.

5. Estimate conversion rates at each stage to track progress, identify bottlenecks, and project revenue accurately.

This documentation enhances tracking, identifies issues, and ultimately leads to increased sales.

Define prospect flow

In the digital era, organizations often use tools like Salesforce, HubSpot, PipeDrive, or Copper CRM to manage their sales process. Regardless of the tool, defining how prospects flow through the process is crucial. Whether using digital platforms or Excel spreadsheets, it's vital to clearly outline each stage and criteria for progression. For instance, starting with the prospecting stage, contacts move through attempted contact, made contact, qualifying, sales meeting, and deal won or lost stages. Naming conventions can vary, but understanding each stage and its criteria ensures efficient prospect progression from initial contact to becoming a new customer.

Define metrics for success

Once you've defined your sales process steps, it's crucial to measure success at each stage to identify bottlenecks and optimize performance. In the prospecting stage, track the total number of prospects and the percentage that qualifies. For connecting or making initial contact, map out quality engagements and determine how many qualify for the next stage. In the qualifying stage, measure the number of leads fitting your qualification standards and those moving on to formal meetings. For the sales meeting stage, track live meetings and consider the average sales cycle. In onboarding, measure the time to get new customers up and running quickly. In follow-up or customer service, establish metrics for proactive check-ins, feedback requests, and referrals. Keep metrics simple for clarity and alignment across the organization, ensuring everyone understands the pipeline, revenue potential, and the path to creating satisfied customers.

What you should know, do, say, and show

The crucial part of a great sales process is the "moments of impact customer conversation" during the sales meeting or customer conversation (step four in our model). This step is the linchpin, and success hinges on how well it's executed. To excel in this phase, you should thoroughly research the prospect's goals, challenges, and business operations. Utilize a clear conversation roadmap that builds personal trust through connection and leverages storytelling focused on the prospect's agenda. Engage in visual storytelling, whether in-person or virtually, and use insightful questions to involve the prospect in the narrative. The key is to ensure that the prospect feels a sense of ownership in the solution you provide. Following these tips will enhance your readiness and contribute to a more positive experience for the prospect, ultimately leading to better outcomes for you.

Chapter 2 Inclusive Selling

What diversity means to the sales marketplace

In the past, sales strategies focused on a single ideal client based on demographics. However, the modern competitive and global economy calls for a shift towards diversification in sales strategies. Embracing inclusion and diversity in sales means recognizing both visible and invisible customer characteristics, such as race, ethnicity, gender, age, culture, education, and more. Inclusive selling involves understanding and respecting the unique backgrounds and perspectives of customers, allowing businesses to tap into new markets and foster expansive growth.

Understanding yourself as it relates to diversity

To leverage the opportunities diversity brings to your sales, start by becoming the most open-minded and quick-learning individual among your peers. Incorporating diversity into your sales practice should be a regular part of your routine. Building relationships is key. Conduct an introspection exercise by recalling situations where you had to understand other cultures or perspectives. Identify commonalities with those individuals to bridge the gap created by the unknown. Uncover shared interests by engaging in conversations and learning about others' passions. Address blind spots arising from biases and prejudices through exposure to different groups. Empty your mind of preconceived notions, ask questions, and discover common ground, realizing that you have more in common with others than differences.

Introspection Exercise:

1. Set a timer for 10 minutes and list situations decoding other cultures.

2. Recall instances like visiting a foreign country or attending events with unfamiliar rules.

3. Reflect on the list and note what felt different and made you uncomfortable.

4. Identify factors causing discomfort and document them.

5. Examine the list again, noting commonalities with those individuals.

6. Embrace basic similarities, such as being human, to bridge differences.

7. Recognize that, upon closer inspection, people share many similarities despite initial differences.

8. Utilize this exercise regularly to enhance self-awareness and understanding of common ground.

What diverse customers are looking for

1. Respectful Treatment: Treat customers with respect by understanding their needs, being available, and valuing them as individuals.

2. Research and Preparation: Prior to meetings, conduct thorough research on customers, their business, and background to demonstrate active listening and personalized care.

3. Tailored Approach: Ask targeted questions based on research to customize your sales pitch, showcasing genuine interest and setting yourself apart.

4. Customer-Centric Solutions: Offer products or services tailored to the specific needs of the customer, avoiding one-size-fits-all approaches.

5. Post-Sale Accountability: Maintain post-sale availability and demonstrate accountability, ensuring customers feel supported and confident in their purchase.

6. Relationship Building: View each sale as the beginning of a relationship, not the end, and consistently back up claims with evidence to foster trust.

7. Repeated Sales: By investing time and effort in understanding and valuing customers, you can establish yourself as a trusted advisor, fostering lifelong relationships and repeated sales.

Research Strategy:

Before entering diverse markets, thorough research is crucial. Gain confidence throughout the sales process with the following insights:

1. Customer's Business:

  - Significant challenges and opportunities

  - Ideal time for purchase

  - Company size, employee count, roles, and operations

2. Customer's Background:

  - Industry entry details

  - Awards, recognitions, volunteerism

  - Community involvement

3. Customer's Culture:

  - Cultural customs, norms, traditions

4. Industry Insights:

  - Dominant players

- Customer's impact and position

- Industry trends and challenges

5. Sales Process Specifics:

  - Decision-making process

  - Key decision-makers and timeline

6. Relationship Dynamics:

  - Personal vs. business focus

7. Communication Preferences:

  - Customer's preferred communication methods

  - Establishing rapport effectively

8. Language Considerations:

  - Need for translated materials

9. Meeting Structure Understanding:

  - Adapt sales meetings based on expectations

10. Body Language Recognition:

   - Understanding signs and signals

11. Social Awareness:

   - Awareness of political, religious, and social beliefs (if applicable)

A comprehensive approach to research ensures a nuanced understanding, facilitating successful engagement in diverse markets.

Understanding yourself as it relates to diversity

In a growing and diverse market, seizing opportunities requires targeting new segments. Overcoming challenges involves strategic tools:

1. Research is Key:

- Prioritize in-depth research on both the overall market and specific target customers.

- Explore market-specific publications for relevant insights.

2. Embrace Open-Mindedness:

- Overcome biases and preconceived notions.

- Practice genuine open-mindedness in both theory and interactions.

3. Practice Makes Perfect:

- Actively engage with the diverse market through regular interactions.

- Gain confidence and understanding through hands-on practice.

4. Build Presence:

- Establish a strong presence in niche markets.

- Gain customer trust by being perceived as actively involved and engaged.

5. Constant Engagement:

- Listen to customer needs, keep promises, and prove reliability.

- Build a solid reputation through consistent engagement in chosen markets.

Success lies in sustained efforts, avoiding a disappearing act, and gradually building a reputation through genuine involvement in diverse markets.

Assess the blind spots that limit your sales opportunities

Broadening your sales strategy opens up new opportunities. An insurance adjuster's experience highlights the blind spots in expectations—challenging stereotypes. Reflect on your strategy:

1. Question Assumptions:

- Identify potential blind spots by assessing preconceived notions about target customers.

- Evaluate your list of potential customers and the words used to describe them.

2. Challenge Comfort Zones:

   - Push beyond comfort zones to uncover diverse opportunities.

   - Consider perspectives beyond your own to ensure a more inclusive approach.

3. Diverse Perspectives:

   - Encourage colleagues to contribute to the list to gain diverse perspectives.

   - Remove biases and explore opportunities through a fresh lens.

By questioning assumptions and challenging comfort zones, you unlock the potential to target a more diverse and expansive customer base.

Common Blind Spots: Unconscious Biases

We all possess blind spots, often unaware of their influence. Recognizing and addressing these biases is crucial. Common blind spots include:

1. Confirmation Blind Spot:

   - Preferring validation over challenges, seeking feedback from those who share your views.

2. Authority Blind Spot:

   - Granting more weight to input from figures of authority, potentially dismissing alternative perspectives.

3. Age Blind Spot:

   - Holding generalized beliefs about age groups, such as assumptions about technology proficiency.

4. Gender Blind Spot:

   - Stereotyping or having preconceived notions about gender roles and perspectives.

5. Regional Blind Spot:

   - Holding biases based on geographic locations, forming assumptions about people from different areas.

6. Bias Blind Spot:

- Believing in minimal bias while failing to recognize one's own blind spots—an inherent paradox.

Understanding and acknowledging these blind spots is essential for fostering empathy and practicing self-awareness. Blind spots are shaped by various factors, emphasizing the need for continuous reflection and learning.

Selling through cultural differences

Understanding and respecting different cultures is crucial for successful sales. Failing to connect with customers on a cultural level can hinder the sales process. To enhance cultural awareness, start with thorough presale research. Familiarize yourself with the do's, don'ts, and taboos of the target culture. If the language differs, learn key phrases. Additionally, grasp the cultural priorities, such as family dynamics, work values, and religious influences.

During sales meetings, remain observant and adaptable. Pay attention to greetings, the importance of casual conversation, and table manners. Despite diligent preparation, cultural nuances may still catch you off guard, as illustrated by a business trip to China where seating arrangements and meal etiquette differed significantly.

Embrace openness and step out of your comfort zone to build rapport. Recognize that cultural differences may challenge you but contribute to establishing trust. An example is the Saudi crown prince and President Bush walking hand in hand, signifying friendship despite being outside Bush's comfort zone. Ultimately, demonstrating sensitivity to your customers' cultures emphasizes that the relationship prioritizes their needs over yours.

How cultural differences manifest themselves when selling

A successful salesperson must adjust their approach to align with the customer's culture. While the U.S. sales culture values extroversion, confidence, and dialogue, this may not be universally effective. Cultural differences impact small talk, formality, attitudes toward competition, personal versus business interactions, and pricing negotiations. In reserved cultures like East Asia and Western Europe, a more formal and polite approach is necessary. Additionally, some cultures prioritize relationships over the best price, and personal demeanor may be perceived differently. Understanding these cultural nuances is essential for effective sales, emphasizing the importance of research and adapting your strategy to each unique cultural context.

Researching Cultural Norms and Traditions:

1. Communication: Understand and adapt to your customer's preferred communication style, considering disabilities, language barriers, and preferred methods/timing, both verbal and nonverbal.

2. Religious/Spiritual Practices: Demonstrate respect and sensitivity to your customer's religious or spiritual practices, being mindful of customs and traditions.

3. Diet: Be aware of dietary limits, preferences, or restrictions for both yourself and your customer during interactions.

4. Blind Spots: Identify and address your own blind spots, recognizing preconceived beliefs or misunderstandings about your customer's background, preferences, or practices.

5. Holidays: Recognize and acknowledge the significance of holidays in your customer's world or community.

6. Your Customs/Practices: Evaluate if there are customs or practices inherent to your identity or culture that might be confusing or offensive to your customers.

Selling through gender differences

Navigating diverse customer demographics, including cultural and generational distinctions, requires reliance on customer research. Despite diminishing gender differences in earnings and positions, it's crucial to remain conscious of nuanced approaches in sales. In the B2C market, recognizing the significant buying power of women is essential. Selling across genders entails distinct considerations. When men sell to women, emphasis shifts from a transactional to a relational approach, focusing on the feel of the deal and the relationship's significance. Women buyers prioritize personalized interactions, cleanliness, and attentive service. Conversely, women selling to men may find success by presenting facts and figures succinctly, as men often value a more straightforward approach. Balancing communication styles is crucial, acknowledging potential perceptions of brevity. Recognizing the unique preferences of individuals within genders is vital, emphasizing curiosity and sensitivity to gender identity dynamics in sales meetings.

Gender Differences in Selling Preferences:

Women's Preferences:

1. Relationship-focused: Women value knowing and being known by the seller.

2. Yes vs. no: Women are drawn to the gains they will experience from the product rather than the losses incurred by not buying.

3. Research-based: Women conduct thorough research, knowing their product needs and what they know about the seller.

4. Long-term focused: Women prioritize long-term benefits and are willing to pay more for lasting gains.

5. Advice/counsel: Women seek and appreciate guidance and expertise throughout the buying process.

Men's Preferences:

1. Make it quick: Men prefer expediting the buying process rather than slowing it down.

2. Advice adverse: While men appreciate input, they prefer less detail compared to women.

3. Easy, easy, easy: Men desire a comfortable and uncomplicated buying process, avoiding unnecessary hurdles.

4. Facts and data: Men value facts and data, which accelerate their decision-making.

5. Control the process: Men often want to control the buying process, determining timing, methods, and overall experience.

Key trends in prospecting across generational differences

To succeed in sales, it's crucial to comprehend and connect with individuals across all generations. Three key generational trends impacting markets are worth noting. First, changing buyer behaviors, particularly among millennials who heavily rely on digital sources, prefer peer input, and emphasize inclusivity. In the B2B market, expect team interactions; in B2C, recognize constant peer communication.

Second, shifting buyer values reveal millennials' focus on sustainability and social responsibility. To appeal to them, align your products with genuine contributions to societal and environmental concerns.

The third trend is changing communication mediums. Tailor your approach based on each generation's preferences. Understand how they gather information and make decisions—Gen Z may prefer social media, millennials respond well to email marketing, and Gen Z might favor YouTube videos.

The fourth trend underscores the importance of presence. Millennials conduct 80% of their research before engaging with a salesperson. Therefore, establishing a strong online presence is vital to being recognized and verified before the first meeting with a prospect. As numerous generations coexist in the marketplace, success hinges on understanding and connecting with people across all age groups.

Selling successfully across generations is a vital skill in today's diverse market. The key demographics include Baby Boomers, Millennials, and the upcoming Generation Z. Baby Boomers, often decision-makers, appreciate traditional sales strategies but value honesty, reliability, and a clear pitch. Millennials, known for research-driven decision-making, seek value aligned with their principles. They prefer collaboration and inclusivity, and a strong online presence is crucial. Generation Z, technologically advanced, requires early and frequent engagement, often virtually.

To appeal to Baby Boomers, prioritize customer research, offer a well-prepared pitch, and emphasize reliability. For those retiring, focus on personal connections, engaging in small talk about their business as a legacy.

When dealing with Millennials, maintain a strong industry presence, be prepared for collaboration, and showcase adaptability. For Generation Z, early and virtual engagement is key, requiring enhanced digital skills.

Success across these generations relies on being a trusted advisor, adapting offerings to customer values, and demonstrating respect. Mastering sales strategies tailored to each generation expands your customer base and doubles sales income.

Selling to people with different beliefs

Successful sales hinge on building rapport and understanding the prospect, even when faced with different belief systems. Addressing challenges tied to beliefs, particularly in areas like religion and politics, is essential for relationship-building and gaining trust. To navigate this, consider the following:

1. Self-reflection: Assess the impact of the customer's belief system on your feelings. Acknowledge any initial biases and evaluate if you can prioritize their needs regardless of differences.

2. Respect: Allow people to hold their beliefs without attempting to change or convince them otherwise. Respect differences without judgment, focusing on understanding clients' challenges and goals.

3. Find common ground: Instead of dwelling on differences, identify shared values or goals. Emphasize commonalities that transcend beliefs, fostering a stronger connection.

4. Non-interference: Prioritize your role as a sales professional supporting clients' growth and goals. If beliefs interfere with your ability to serve the client, consider referring them to a colleague who can better address their needs.

Approaching diverse beliefs with honesty, respect, a focus on common ground, and a commitment to non-interference can transform challenges into opportunities for growth and understanding in sales relationships.

Understanding the entire sales process

Selling to emerging market segments is a long-term strategy crucial for adapting to a dynamic market. Diversifying customers, especially minorities and women, requires attentive presale efforts. Research thoroughly, ask informed questions, and be sensitive to cultural differences. The sale itself, though relatively quick, demands adaptability to customer needs and backgrounds. Post-sale, building a strong post-purchase relationship is vital in a growing market with increasing competition. Establishing yourself as indispensable through reliability, trustworthiness, and a human connection position you as a trusted advisor, securing long-term relationships and referrals. This approach ensures continued success in selling to diverse customer bases.

Chapter 3 Asking Great Sales Questions

Understand your customer's business

It may seem logical on the surface to ask a series of questions to uncover opportunities and then present a solution, the needs analysis often feels like an interrogation to the prospect. This is due to the prospect's self-preservation instincts and the perception that it leads to a sales pitch. To avoid falling into the needs analysis trap, thorough preparation is essential. Conduct research on the prospect, utilizing tools like LinkedIn to gather information on their name, title, work history, education, and more. Additionally, explore a company details such as size, revenue, mission, and industry trends. Familiarize yourself with the prospect's selling message to gain insights into their goals and challenges. By approaching sales meetings with specific, problem-centric, and relevant questions, you demonstrate empathy and enhance credibility. This proactive and informed approach sets you apart from salespeople who rely on superficial knowledge and ask basic questions. Invest the time to prepare and structure meaningful questions tailored to your prospect and their business, making a significant difference in your sales approach.

Understand your customer's role

Knowing your customer's role goes beyond surface-level details like their name and title. Understanding how their role aligns with the company's strategic plan, supports growth, and faces pressures from higher-ups provides valuable insights. Customers in similar roles within an industry share common goals and challenges. Deepening your understanding enables you to relate to their daily activities, leading to more meaningful questions that address their concerns. The benefits of truly understanding your customer's role include clear focus, staying problem-centric, using appropriate language, fostering empathy, and strategic positioning. This comprehensive knowledge positions you as an expert and trusted advisor, enhancing your ability to provide tailored solutions and build lasting relationships. Investing the extra effort to understand your customer's role makes you a more empathetic and effective salesperson, driving connection, credibility, and ultimately, success.

Understand your customer's objectives

Once you've gained a comprehensive understanding of your prospect's business and empathized with their role, the next step is delving deeper. Human decision-making is rooted in self-preservation, with urgency to avoid loss twice as powerful as the drive to achieve gain. According to Nobel laureates Kahneman and Tversky, customers are focused on solving problems rather than buying products. To ask pertinent questions, grasp your customer's top three to five goals and the corresponding challenges that could hinder their achievement. Identify the risks that matter to them. For instance, VPs of sales in Fortune 1000 B2B companies commonly aim to increase revenue, decrease sales cycles, minimize discounting, reduce turnover, and enhance profitability. Your questions should pinpoint problems aligning with these goals. For example, if you provide field-based sales manager coaching software, inquire about challenges related to revenue targets and persistent discounting. This approach captures their attention by addressing what truly matters to them, fostering engagement and urgency to solve their concerns.

The importance of why

To build trust, it's crucial to recognize that people buy from those they trust, like, and connect with. While many attempt rapport-building, the typical approach often lacks authenticity. Mere observations, such as commenting on a picture, don't establish a genuine connection. Research indicates that our subconscious evaluates interactions through a risk lens, categorizing individuals as potential friends or foes. To foster trust, share an authentic and meaningful story, revealing your beliefs and why you do what you do. By opening with a personal narrative, like the "My Why Story," you create a foundation of mutual trust, making it easier to ask challenging questions and engage customers honestly.

Connection vs. credibility

To gain the privilege of posing status quo challenging questions, it's crucial to build trust, which comes in two forms: personal and professional. Personal trust involves creating a genuine connection through qualities like humility, authenticity, honesty, and appropriate vulnerability. Professional trust is established by showcasing credibility through knowledge, skills, and capability. To engage prospects effectively, strike a balance between personal connection and professional credibility, ensuring your questions align with their goals and challenges.

Confirm goals

Human beings, including your customers, operate from a self-preservation perspective, focusing on goals and potential threats. It's crucial to understand and confirm your customers' primary goals, steering clear of overly granular inquiries. For instance, selling programs to executives, identify overarching goals like revenue growth, increased profitability, shorter sales cycles, and a high-performance culture. During prospect conversations, strategically confirm these high-level goals in the customers' words, emphasizing their agenda. This not only establishes connection and credibility but also allows you to create urgency around solving problems that jeopardize these primary goals. Prioritize understanding your customers' top three to four overarching goals before meeting, presenting these goals to drive connection and credibility. By setting the goalpost and guiding the conversation, you position yourself as the solution provider for the problems affecting their goals.

Prioritize goals

After confirming your customer's top three to four primary goals, assess their feelings about goal prioritization. Customers prioritize goals based on potential risks and impacts on business success. For instance, a VP of sales may prioritize goals like revenue growth, increased profitability, shorter sales cycles, and reduced turnover. Knowing their priority order is crucial for effective solution positioning. When asking questions, demonstrate credibility by outlining typical goals, introduce a problem, and inquire about their perspective and goal priority. Don't just ask about goals; do your homework, suggest top goals, introduce insightful risks, and then ask them to react and prioritize. This intentional sequence effectively engages the buying brain.

Use insights

Earn the right to ask questions by framing them around what your prospect cares about using insights. Insights are relevant pieces of information or third-party data points that highlight a problem or issue. Instead of a traditional needs analysis, leverage insights to pose insightful questions. Instead of directly asking about sales issues, use insights to provoke a question, such as, "Do you feel your sales team has any gaps in differentiating your solutions to ideal customers?" Using insights makes the problem seem widespread, increasing the likelihood of obtaining comprehensive answers. Preparation is key; create three to four questions for each insight to integrate them naturally into your conversation.

Quantify the problem

To ensure prospects see value in the questioning process, share insights and validate the specific impact for them through effective questions. For example, if a survey reveals that 58% of qualified deals end in a no decision, ask the prospect if their experience aligns with this data. Once they provide their perspective, quantify the impact. If they, for instance, say 30% of their deals end in no decision, proceed to ask about their average deal value and monthly deal volume. By multiplying the percentage by deal value, you can show the prospect that the 30 deals represent $300,000 in lost monthly revenue. Highlighting a modest 10% improvement as potentially adding $30,000 to their bottom line creates a tangible sense of urgency. This questioning model allows prospects to quantify the problem's impact in their own terms, making them more receptive to seeking solutions.

Personalize the impact

Human beings are inherently driven by self-preservation, and this biological instinct influences our decision-making. In the context of effective sales questioning, it's crucial to engage the customer's brain by highlighting the personal impact of a problem. Instead of focusing solely on product features, employ a customer-centric approach that addresses their individual concerns. For instance, in the health insurance sector targeting HR leaders, emphasize issues like turnover and employee satisfaction. Use third-party insights to frame questions that resonate emotionally with the buyer. This strategy encourages customers to share personal experiences, providing valuable insights for tailoring solutions to their specific needs.

Map the solution to the problem

The challenge arises when we label our products as solutions but primarily describe them in terms of features, inundating customers with facts and data. The emphasis has been on asking insightful questions to grasp customer goals and understand the contextual problems hindering those goals. Once alignment is achieved on recognized problems, the transition to presenting solutions should be conversational and led by clarifying questions. When introducing features, such as an HR software system's time-tracking capability, connect it explicitly to a previously acknowledged problem. This approach not only simplifies the solution but also reinforces its problem-solving effectiveness. Each feature presentation should end with a clarifying question to ensure the customer recognizes the solution's direct relevance to their identified problem, fostering personal investment in its implementation.

Define the value

When considering the concept of value, it's crucial to understand how both you and your customers perceive it. Miriam Webster defines value as the relative worth, utility, or importance of something, often quantified through calculation or measurement. Notably, customer value is seen as a significant solution to a problem, the cost of which is much less than the expense associated with the problem itself. This distinction is vital; focusing on your product in a transactional manner invites comparison with competing products, leading to pricing pressure. Instead, emphasize that your solution offers savings compared to the high cost of the underlying problem. Asking insightful questions about value initiates early in the customer conversation, helping define the problem and its associated costs.

For instance, discussing an HR solution's time and attendance feature involves quantifying the cost of lost productivity due to unscheduled breaks. By the end of the conversation, the customer can articulate the value based on the defined problems and their costs. This step is arguably more crucial than presenting the solution itself. For instance, in an HR software example, identifying the costs associated with various features could quickly total significant monthly value. When presenting your solution, connecting each feature to a defined problem allows you to demonstrate the substantial value of solving multiple issues with a solution that costs significantly less. This approach not only defines the value of your solution but also empowers the customer to logically and naturally decide to implement it. The key is aligning the solution's cost with the perceived value of solving the identified problems.

Partnership agreements

Sales philosophies from past decades often promoted aggressive closing techniques, epitomized by the "Always Be Closing" (ABC) mantra. However, this approach, while providing short-term success for some, contributed to the negative perception of sales. Modern sales professionals, irrespective of their industry, recognize the counterproductivity of such tactics. Trust is the cornerstone of successful sales, and constant hard closes erode that trust. Do not rely on a trusted advisor that doesn't engage in traditional closing. Instead, a brain trusts certified sales professional, having built a partnership with the customer, respectfully guides them toward the next steps in the process. Partnership agreements emphasize the mutual investment and shared commitment in finding a solution. The recommended approach involves a simple question, acknowledging the joint effort required and respecting the customer's role in the partnership. This strategy, rooted in connection, credibility, and respect, allows customers to choose to solve their problems, fostering a positive and trust-based relationship.

Chapter 4 Analytics-Driven Storytelling

Comfort in numbers

In business, we often find comfort in numbers, seeking certainty in data. However, presenting extensive data without a clear storyline can overwhelm and confuse the audience. Analytics, while crucial, should be viewed as supporting elements in a larger story. Stories engage our primal instincts, making information memorable and impactful. To achieve the ultimate goal of motivating action, it's essential to integrate analytics into a compelling narrative. Reflect on past presentations with data and consider how incorporating a clear story could enhance impact and achieve better results.

Transforming from analyst to storyteller

Being a numbers person can hinder effective communication, as relying solely on data may not engage the audience. To overcome this, it's crucial to shift your mindset and integrate storytelling with analytics. While analytics appeal to the logical left brain, stories tap into the creative right brain, resulting in more comprehensive communication. Although telling stories may feel uncomfortable, practicing and detaching from spreadsheets are essential for success. Taking the risk of storytelling transforms your communication style, requiring patience and practice to become comfortable. Start by telling a daily story to someone, evaluate the engagement, and make improvements for continuous enhancement. Embrace the transformative journey of incorporating storytelling into your communication approach.

The simple formula for a great story

- Effective storytelling isn't about complex structures; it's about connecting your problem, solution, and audience. Forget overly complicated formulas; simplicity is key. Focus on four essential elements: setting (normal situation), problem (challenge uncovered through analytics), climax (critical point with potential consequences), and resolution (recommendation or action). Apply these elements to recent presentations with analytics to create a more powerful and engaging narrative.

The problem reveals your story

Effective storytelling with analytics is not about entertainment; it's about solving problems or guiding the audience toward solutions. Utilizing a process called sales design thinking helps set up analytics-driven problem-solving. Rather than relying solely on a problem statement, incorporating challenge questions that delve deeper into the situation is more beneficial. A case example of a company facing a sales performance issue demonstrates the shift from a simple problem statement to a more complex challenge question. By asking specific questions about what happened, how, when, who was involved, where, and why, a more refined challenge question emerged, directing focus toward communication, collaboration, and predictable revenue growth instead of simple incentives. The exercise encourages revisiting and refining the original problem statement to uncover deeper insights.

Have a goal for your story

After formulating your challenge question from the problem statement, consider the specific action you want your audience to take as a result of your story. Avoid the trap of overwhelming with excessive analytics; focus on the desired action for your audience. Tailor your approach based on your audience, whether executives, customers, or internal teams, and clearly define the action you seek. Anticipate potential questions that may arise from your story, enhancing your preparedness and response.

What's a storytelling campaign?

A storytelling campaign is about connecting your storyline with your audience. To effectively convey your message, consider multiple audiences, tailor messages for each, provide proof sources to back up claims, choose suitable communication vehicles, and plan the timing and frequency of your messages. Recognize that different audiences may require different approaches and messages. Craft your campaign with a focus on simplicity, ensuring your message is clear and impactful. Reflect on a message you need to communicate, and structure a campaign using these five components: audience, message, proof source, vehicle, and timing.

A strategic view of your data story

Utilizing a business model aids in comprehending options and focusing efforts. Models provide a structured approach, saving time by building on existing knowledge. The Revenue Roadmap is a useful model, analyzing insight, sales strategy, customer coverage, and enablement. Each component is interconnected, requiring a holistic perspective. Embrace a model to enhance understanding, gain context, and accelerate problem-solving. Evaluate your current project using the Revenue Roadmap, identifying its place in the model and considering related disciplines for a comprehensive solution.

The Revenue Roadmap is a conceptual model used to guide businesses in understanding and optimizing their growth strategies. It encompasses various interconnected components that contribute to revenue generation.

1. Insight:

 - Focus: Understand the market, customers, competitors, and internal business dynamics.

 - Components: Market research, customer feedback, competitive analysis, and business performance metrics.

2. Sales Strategy:

 - Focus: Develop a strategic approach to selling, including product offerings, target customer segments, value proposition, and market approach.

 - Components: Product/service portfolio, segmentation and targeting, value proposition development, and Go-to-Market strategy.

3. Customer Coverage:

 - Focus: Implement the sales strategy by defining how the company interacts with customers, which channels are used, and how the sales force operates.

 - Components: Sales channels, sales roles, sales process, rules of engagement, and territory management.

4. Enablement:

- Focus: Provide the necessary support, tools, and resources to ensure effective execution of the sales strategy and customer coverage plan.

- Components: Incentive compensation, sales training and development, technology and tools, and support programs.

Your analytics players

As you craft your story, remember that analytics play a supporting role, not the main characters. They can be introduced at different points—setting, problem, climax, or resolution. For example, consider a company's growth trajectory in the test and measurement equipment business. The healthy growth seen in years one to five sets the stage, but the problem arises as quotas outpace growth. The climax emerges as average quota attainment declines, signaling a potential failure to meet growth objectives. Another example focuses on sales strategy, revealing that moderate growth in year two results from customer retention and penetration, but high churn and reliance on current customers pose a future problem. These analytics can become integral parts of your story, enhancing the narrative beyond raw data. So, choose three favorite analytics from recent reports and envision how they contribute to the storyline's setting, problem, climax, or resolution. Transition from mere analytics to a compelling narrative.

Connect the dots with data

Connect the dots between your challenge question, your findings, and the desired action from your audience. This is where your work and process analytics converge, and you need to extract the story from the data. Remember, the story isn't everything in your analytics; it's often hidden within them. Avoid backward engineering—don't force a preconceived story. Your discovered story may differ from expectations, adding a touch of magic to the process. Be prepared to set aside other analytics once you find your story, ensuring clarity is maintained. An illustrative example from Sales Globe involves survey data on the return to work and pandemic impacts. From a vast dataset, a compelling story emerged: 62% of people worked remotely during the pandemic, with 77% wanting to continue part-time. However, companies expected only 36% to work remotely, leading to a conflict. Additionally, 34% of employees would quit if forced to return, creating turnover risks. Further analysis revealed an innovation gap, with only 45% of companies investing in collaboration beyond basic video. The resolution? A need for a back-to-work plan focusing on retention and innovation. This condensed, impactful story was shared with company leaders, resonating with their experiences. Now, apply this approach to one of your recent data-rich reports. Identify the most impactful storyline within the analytics, focusing on the resolution point and assessing its enhanced message power compared to the initial data overload.

Refine your story

A concise and impactful story is more memorable than a lengthy one. Less is more when it comes to analytics storytelling. As someone who tends to hoard analytics, it's crucial to overcome this habit for clearer communication. The top five reasons for being an analytics hoarder include the desire to showcase hard work, appear intelligent, mask insecurities, avoid making a clear recommendation, and insufficient time for message refinement. Embracing the rule of threes, a powerful simplification method, is crucial. Comedy often utilizes this rule, creating memorable and concise stories. Apply the rule of threes to your past presentations or information-laden emails to enhance their impact by distilling them down to three essential elements.

Engage the outsider

In the process of crafting both analytical and creative stories, it's crucial to delve deeply into the subject. However, excessive focus can lead to losing perspective, making the input of an outsider invaluable. An outsider provides an objective viewpoint, offering a different context, challenging your thinking, and aiding in preparation for presentations. Outsiders, unburdened by the same constraints and distractions, can identify aspects that might be overlooked. Although the intrusion of an outsider may not always be welcomed amid the hectic finalization of a presentation, their fresh perspective is essential for achieving clarity. The outsider, ideally someone with a fresh outlook, knowledge of the content, and good thinking skills, can be a boss, associate, business coach, or friend. Involving them at key points, such as when formulating the challenge question, analyzing analytics findings, and finalizing the story, is beneficial. The outsider can provide individual input or participate in a brain trust, reading material in advance and offering valuable, free-form insights. Embrace the outsider's input for refinement, and witness the enhanced quality of your narrative. For an upcoming significant presentation, identify one or two outsiders, share the material beforehand, schedule a meeting with them, and commit to harnessing the power of the outsider's perspective.

Hone and master your data story

The key here is practice. Practicing storytelling enhances your skills as an analytics storyteller. Extend your practice beyond analytics stories; tell various types of stories, preferably shorter ones, whenever possible. Testing your story is crucial, as creating and telling it are distinct. Transition to active storytelling by speaking instead of writing. Initially, tell the story to yourself and record it to assess your presentation style. Gradually reduce visual aids and scripts to reinforce the message in your memory. Begin with low-risk practice, engaging with someone familiar to build comfort with articulating your points and hearing your voice. For a more advanced level, consider seeking external assistance, such as a speaking or acting coach. To boost your confidence, take a report you're working on, set aside the pencil, turn on the camera, and tell your story multiple times, observing improvements in your comfort and confidence levels.

Develop your storytelling style

While practicing, your unique style and persona will naturally emerge. Embrace your authentic self, as genuine speakers connect best with audiences. If you're excellent with numbers but a bit awkward, it's okay—authenticity resonates. Look for role models who align with parts of your desired presentation style. A valuable tip is to study stand-up comedians for presentation techniques, adapting them while staying true to yourself. Embrace your quirks, as they make you relatable and human. Engage in an exercise: share your story with someone you know, seeking feedback on authenticity and comfort. Gradually refine your delivery until it feels natural, highlighting what makes you special.

Make storytelling your lifelong hobby

Embrace storytelling as a lifelong hobby, aiming for gradual improvement rather than immediate mastery. Treat it like learning a language—practice leads to fluency. Patience is crucial; don't rush the process. A seasoned storyteller advised approaching it as a long-term pursuit, focusing on continuous improvement. Lowering expectations makes the journey more manageable. Recognize that proficiency takes time and practice. Amid a world of short-term goals, permit yourself the necessary time to evolve into a great analytic storyteller. Cultivate storytelling as a lifelong passion.

Chapter 5 Handling Objections

The buyer and seller relationship

Often, we view the sales and buying process as adversarial, perceiving buyers as resistant to our offerings. This mindset can lead to negativity and hinder successful interactions. Recognizing the buyer's challenging role in making impactful decisions, salespeople should prioritize building trust from the outset. Trust is fostered by comprehensive product knowledge, thorough business understanding, efficient use of time, attentive listening, and unwavering credibility and integrity. Successful interactions hinge on a mutual understanding that objections and clarifications are integral to the sales process, fostering collaboration rather than an "us versus them" mentality.

The presentation and the sales call

Success in sales requires a thorough adherence to a sales process, ensuring full preparedness for buyer interactions. Neglecting any step may lead to unhandled objections, risking a lost sale. Prioritizing planning and preparation, instilled by experienced sales managers, remains a crucial message for training new sales professionals. While presenting products or services, anticipating and addressing potential objections is paramount. Focus on understanding the buyer and thoroughly grasping the strengths and weaknesses of your offering through comprehensive research. This diligent approach allows salespeople to navigate objections confidently, contributing to consistent revenue achievement.

A plan to handle sales objections

Anticipating objections is integral to successful sales presentations, though facing objections can still be challenging. Acknowledging our human reactions, like frustration, when objections arise is normal. However, responding strategically is crucial for a productive outcome. Take a moment to breathe and write down the objection for thoughtful consideration. Ask clarifying questions to understand the buyer's perspective, maintaining composure and patience. Avoid turning objections into debates; instead, respond confidently and honestly, addressing concerns directly. Disagree tactfully if needed, emphasizing professionalism throughout. Handling objections skillfully transforms this phase into a pivotal aspect of your sales call.

How to develop your strategy for handling objections

To succeed in sales, follow your training framework but adapt it to your style. While topics like pipeline tracking and presentation formats are straightforward, prospecting, closing, and handling objections invite diverse opinions. Unlike some aggressive approaches, I emphasize hard work and continuous improvement. Handling objections is crucial, and I identify five common ones: money, contentment, decision authority, product uncertainty, and timing. Your approach may differ, but my goal is to inspire reflection, evaluation, and enhancement of your personalized, successful sales method. Constantly seek new techniques to prospect, close deals, and adeptly handle objections throughout your sales career.

Sales objection one: Price or budget

As the regional sales representative for an IT training company, you've been in contact with John Evans, Learning and Development Manager, for three months. However, in a recent meeting, John raises a pricing objection, expressing concerns about the expense. Anticipating such objections is crucial. In responding, focus on extracting more information, emphasize the value of your service, and be cautious about immediate price negotiations. Address John's concerns by isolating the objection and offering solutions, such as stage rollouts or flexible invoicing. Preparation and belief in your service are key to collaboratively resolving price or budget issues during sales opportunities.

Sales objection two: Features, benefits, and trust

Breaking into the buying programs of a national consumer packaged goods company in your territory is challenging but lucrative. During a 15-minute introduction, the buyer calmly states that the current product's features and benefits are outstanding, creating a common objection. Overcoming this objection involves four key factors. First, focus on building trust and credibility with the buyer, emphasizing the importance of a strong relationship. Second, know your customer by conducting thorough research before each meeting to anticipate challenges. Third, understand your competition, asking about the features and benefits that matter most to the buyer. Finally, emphasize your product's features and benefits, tailoring them to meet the buyer's needs and demonstrating improvement over the current offering. Overcoming objections requires trust, knowledge, awareness of the competition, and effective presentation of your product's value.

Sales objection three: Decision-making process

You've secured an appointment with Patrica Myers, the business manager of a regional office in your territory. The presentation went well, but Patrica states she lacks the final authority to make the purchase decision. This objection is common but requires strategic handling. First, effective research before the meeting should have revealed potential obstacles like this. Understanding the customer type and their buying procedures is crucial. If Patrica isn't the decision-maker, inquire about who holds that role and seek an introduction. Avoid relying solely on the buyer to discuss your offering with others; aim to present directly to decision-makers. Request assistance from Patrica to meet with other decision-makers, though be mindful of potential delays in committee scenarios. Overcoming objections related to authority or committees underscores the importance of thorough research and understanding the customer's buying process.

Sales objection four: Buyer doesn't want to change

After securing an appointment with Jenny Parker, the purchasing director at Global Dynamics, she expresses that she doesn't want to make a change right now. This common objection may stem from various reasons. If Jenny is concerned about shaking things up due to slowed revenue growth, focus on financial benefits and ease of implementation. If she mentions satisfaction with a competitor, ask about key factors and showcase how your offering excels. If in a contract, inquire about the contract's end date; if it's within six months, consider a follow-up presentation or early contract termination incentives. When Jenny states she's happy with the current situation, address potential complacency by demonstrating a painless change and emphasizing how it enhances her image with management. Investigate objections to tailor a focused comparison showcasing your value.

Sales objection five: No thanks or I'll get back to you

After securing an appointment with Patrick Cooper, the purchasing manager, and presenting your products, Patrick responds with either "No thanks" or "I'll get back to you." These common responses, more critical during the presentation stage, indicate a potential derailment of your message. To salvage the opportunity, directly inquire about Patrick's change in interest. For "No thanks," ask what you missed and clarify your presentation points. For "I'll get back to you," suggest scheduling another meeting to delve into specifics about your value proposition. These non-confrontational questions foster dialogue and help understand and address the underlying issues, allowing you to salvage the opportunity.

Some of the many other sales objections

Common objections from buyers, such as pricing, budget, or decision-making authority, are expected, but encountering unique objections is inevitable. Always be prepared with a professional response. When faced with an unfamiliar objection, follow these three steps: pause to gather thoughts, write down the objection for clarity, and ask a follow-up question for clarification. Examples of unique objections include competitors questioning your service quality—respond with assurance and offer customer recommendations. For objections like being too busy, suggest ways to accommodate their schedule. When requested features pose a challenge, seek more details before committing. Surprising objections, like a buyer's unexpected promotion, require positive acknowledgment and a strategic response to keep the sales process on track. The key is anticipating diverse objections and having a prepared strategy to address them professionally.

How to make the call in a stalled sale

As sales professionals, persistence is crucial, but recognizing when to pivot is equally vital for effective pipeline management. Obstacles and objections are part of the sales process, but being tenacious doesn't mean clinging to stalled opportunities indefinitely. Know your customers, be adaptable, and seek help when needed. Regularly assess revenue assumptions and prioritize time wisely, distinguishing between significant opportunities and small deals that may impede progress. Analyze time allocation for pending deals—consider if efforts elsewhere could be more fruitful. Maintain communication with customers, avoid burning bridges, and always secure a follow-up date. While persistence is key, knowing when to redirect energy is a skill critical for achieving sales goals.

The five responsibilities of a sales professional

Top priorities in sales include thorough planning and preparation, encompassing customer and competitor research, as well as understanding buyers beforehand to anticipate objections. Comprehensive knowledge of your product or service, including strengths, weaknesses, and potential queries, is essential. Distinguishing average salespeople from exceptional ones are skills in closing deals and fulfilling promises. After addressing objections, timely and effective solicitation of business is crucial. Improved communication, reporting, and sharing experiences using CRMs enhance collective learning within a sales team. Continuous learning is imperative, ensuring adaptation and improvement in sales techniques over time. These responsibilities not only enhance credibility but also contribute to building a positive reputation with buyers, enabling the mastery of objection-handling skills.

The ongoing process

Navigating a sales career is challenging, involving tough days of prospecting, pipeline development, and preparing for sales calls. Facing objections from buyers is inevitable but requires anticipation, addressing concerns, and redirecting focus on the product or service offering. Continuous improvement is crucial; learning from peers, engaging in role-playing, and consistently refining objection-handling techniques contribute to sustained success. Accepting that training is never complete is vital for sales professionals consistently achieving their targets.

Chapter 6 Sales Negotiation

The false assumption behind compromise

Steve and Vicky found themselves in a deadlock, refusing to compromise, resembling either power brokers negotiating a multimillion-dollar real estate deal or bickering five-year-olds in a sandbox. The analogy highlights the universal nature of negotiation dynamics, which we start learning early in life. However, traditional compromise, often taught as a resolution tactic, is ineffective, particularly in sales situations. It leads to short-term gains but damages relationships and future deals. Instead, the speaker proposes a more strategic approach, urging negotiators to embrace a noble purpose mindset. This involves understanding the buyer's true goals and fostering a collaborative, solution-oriented conversation, breaking away from win-lose mentalities. The key to success lies in embracing the "power of and" and becoming comfortable with uncertainty. The middle ground, or the place of uncertainty, becomes the creative space for negotiating mutually beneficial solutions, requiring a shift in mindset and language to engage buyers in strategic conversations.

How to start a negotiation with noble purpose

Your ultimate purpose as a seller is to help your client achieve their goals, ensuring a lasting negotiation outcome. Distinguishing between buying criteria and true business objectives is crucial. As a seller, your task is to authentically communicate and understand your buyer's genuine business objectives, emphasizing the importance of a good relationship and mutual trust. Pricing negotiations often become challenging when insightful questions are not asked early in the process. To build a case for value, ask questions about the impact on the buyer's business, its role in the larger picture, alignment with job priorities, and effects on peers, company, subordinates, or boss. The goal is to establish the financial and non-financial impact of the purchase, co-creating value in the uncertain middle ground. Early clarity on buyer goals reduces the likelihood of descending into a price war during negotiations. The powerful early question, "How can we ensure you get everything you need out of this deal?" may initially intimidate salespeople, but it is essential. It prompts buyers to articulate their needs, allowing sellers to address concerns and guide discussions beyond price, ensuring a comprehensive understanding of buyer goals.

Why uncertainty is your ally

Salespeople often find uncertainty uncomfortable as it triggers a threat response in the brain. The desire for certainty is innate as it provides a sense of stability and security. While uncertainty may be challenging, embracing it is crucial for creativity and successful negotiation. Uncertainty doesn't imply lack of balance or planning; it's about not knowing precisely how a situation will unfold. To navigate uncertainty, trust in oneself and the buyer is essential. Rushing to close deals quickly may hinder creativity and lead to a price-focused approach. Being comfortable with some degree of uncertainty allows for asking insightful questions that establish value and avoid price wars. Verbalizing buyer goals and emphasizing value over low prices authentically affirms commitment and increases the likelihood of creating mutually beneficial outcomes. Embracing uncertainty opens the door to a higher brain space where more valuable solutions can be discovered.

The three kinds of negotiations

A victory mindset hinders effective negotiation as it leads to defensive strategies, leaving value on the table. Three types of negotiators include the "churn and burn," focused on closing at any cost; the "in it to win it," employing testimonials and flashy descriptions; and the "lasting value," prioritizing listening and building lasting value. Sellers find the most success as "lasting value" negotiators, demonstrating genuine intentions early and consistently. Despite the willingness to trust being inherent, buyers may misinterpret sellers, necessitating transparent communication to build trust and enhance relationships. A successful negotiation rests on trust, understanding, and a focus on mutual benefit.

When to negotiate and when not to

Recognizing when to negotiate is crucial. Consider Steve, a software salesperson facing repeated post-deal negotiations. Typically, negotiation issues arise from factors earlier in the relationship. Three scenarios where negotiation is ill-advised are: dealing with a non-decision maker, when the product doesn't align, or when the value is established. To address the first scenario, inquire subtly about decision-making involvement early on. If faced with a non-decision maker later, insist on meeting with the actual decision maker before proceeding. In the second scenario, if the buyer claims not to need all features, assess if it's a tactic or a genuine mismatch. If the latter, shift focus from pricing and features to discussing what would be valuable for the buyer. The third scenario involves a buyer rushing the deal, signaling potential loss of value. Only negotiate when dealing with the right decision maker and when the value is established; otherwise, more selling is required.

Four reasons deals fall apart

Deals often fall apart for five main reasons. Firstly, "smoke and mirrors" occur when the buyer has no genuine intention to buy but seeks a lower price from their current vendor. Asking about their current provider and reasons for considering a change can reveal their seriousness. Secondly, undisclosed contract terms can surprise the buyer during negotiations. Ensure all details are communicated before asking for a signature. The third reason is a failure to ask for the close, assuming the deal is lost when the buyer requests something unfeasible. If value is provided, it's acceptable to ask for the close. Fourthly, unclear identified buyers in committee scenarios, common in large companies, can result in deals not progressing. Preemptively identify committee members, objectives, and approval processes. Lastly, insufficiently demonstrated value can lead to perceived high costs. Address this by showcasing the investment's worth to avoid deal failure. Analyze past failed deals to identify patterns and make necessary adjustments for continuous improvement.

How to tell the difference between a buyer and negotiator

To sell major deals successfully, it's crucial to prioritize interactions with buyers rather than negotiators. While negotiators focus solely on securing lower prices, buyers have broader goals and consider value. Identifying the type of person early in the buying process is essential. Clues such as job titles, body language, and the opening of the meeting can provide insights. Questions like who else should be involved, the need for agreement from other parties, and the primary contact for the account can help determine the role of the individual. If dealing with a negotiator, emphasize the importance of involving other stakeholders and meeting with senior leaders to ensure the solution aligns with strategic objectives. For complex, high-value offerings to large companies, involving purchasing or procurement may be necessary without alienating them. The key is to create value throughout the process as a noble purpose seller.

Negotiation in action: Discussing price without value

Reality TV has exposed us to various negotiation techniques, and your buyers likely possess some level of negotiation training. In this scenario featuring Emily, a new sales rep negotiating with Charlie, an experienced purchasing agent, one common buyer tactic is to focus solely on lowering the price without discussing value. Emily adeptly steers the conversation back to value, emphasizing the alignment of goals and objectives. As Charlie persists on the bottom line, Emily highlights the potential impact on service quality if the price is reduced too much. Recognizing Charlie's pressure, instead of immediately defending the value, Emily suggests collaborating on a better value story and involving others in the decision-making process. This approach shifts the dynamic, prompting Charlie to consider the idea of bringing in additional stakeholders. Overall, the key is to navigate the negotiation by balancing value discussion and addressing the buyer's concerns.

Negotiation in action: Belittling value to reduce price

Buyers often employ the tactic of belittling your value early in the conversation, attempting to highlight perceived weaknesses. In this scenario, Charlie challenges the product's credibility, referencing negative reviews and past failures. Emily initially defends the product, emphasizing positive aspects. To break the stalemate, she shifts focus to Charlie's specific concerns, prompting him to reconsider and acknowledge potential impacts on his implementation. By asking insightful questions, Emily uncovers that Charlie's objections were more of a tactic than genuine concerns, demonstrating the importance of curiosity and steering the conversation back to value.

Negotiation in action: Inserting the boss at the last minute

When faced with new information or individuals in the process, be curious and ask questions before attempting to navigate the situation. As a purpose-driven sales negotiator, aim to elevate the conversation for a big win. Buyers may employ a tactic of acting as the decision maker but later introducing their boss. In this scenario, Emily handles it by suggesting involving the boss and emphasizing the importance of understanding her values. When the buyer resists, Emily proposes a brief phone call, successfully navigating the situation with skills to disarm negotiation tactics. The goal is to reduce defensiveness and enhance the overall win rate, recognizing that not every sale will close.

When to use your boss and when to ask for their boss

Knowing how to leverage your boss is crucial in negotiations. Use your boss to connect with the buyer's boss early on by framing it as a standard procedure for key leaders to meet. Additionally, involve your boss in strategic conversations when facing a stalemate, briefing them on the buyer's true objectives and the competitive landscape. Bringing in your boss for critical deals is a valuable resource.

How to diffuse anger without giving away the store

When faced with someone's anger in negotiations, it's important not to internalize it. Instead, practice deep breathing to stay calm. Pause and allow the anger to dissipate naturally. Uncover the underlying issues by asking open-ended questions to understand their perspective. Validate their anger by expressing understanding without becoming defensive. Maintain eye contact and communicate calmly to address the concerns. Never reciprocate anger, and avoid taking it personally; often, the anger is about the issue, not you. Know when to walk away if the person consistently exhibits unreasonable behavior. As a noble purpose negotiator, your goal is to bring out the best in yourself and your buyer, holding space for resolution and understanding. Remember, anger is not permanent.

What to do when your buyer has the Internet in their hand

The internet has transformed the sales landscape, with 70% of the buyer's journey now occurring online. Buyers are well-informed about products, reviews, and pricing before engaging with salespeople. While this may seem challenging, it presents an opportunity for salespersons to focus on value and tailor conversations. Leveraging the wealth of information available online, salespeople should understand buyers' backgrounds, organizational goals, and strategic priorities. Rather than asking basic questions, guide the conversation toward value by acknowledging the buyer's research and probing for specific areas of interest. The internet has enhanced the quality of conversations by providing a foundation of knowledge for both buyers and sellers. Embrace transparency and use your role as a high-value resource in the buyer's journey. Ethical practices are crucial in this age of transparency, as any deceitful behavior will likely be exposed and negatively impact your reputation.

How to negotiate via email

Engaging in email negotiations can lead to misunderstandings and conflicts. Drawing from personal experience as a church board president, the speaker highlights the potential for miscommunication and the absence of respectful communication in emails, despite the church's values. Advising against negotiating via email, the speaker emphasizes the value of in-person or phone negotiations. If compelled to use email, maintaining a gracious tone and avoiding assumptions are crucial. Graciousness involves considering the emotional context and being mindful of the tone in emails. Recognizing the limitations of written communication, the speaker encourages sellers to convey subtle cues through words. Practical tips include crafting specific subject lines, providing warm contextual details, avoiding overthinking, and thorough proofreading before sending emails.

How late is too late to negotiate?

George Flint's quote, "It's never too late to be what you might have been," doesn't always apply to business deals. In specific situations, despite significant investment, it's crucial to recognize sunk costs and cut losses. Sunk costs can cloud judgment, leading to poor decisions and last-minute disappointments. Signs of a failing deal include canceled meetings, lack of urgency, negative body language, praise for competitors, continual delays, and repeated proposal revisions. Rather than dwelling on past investment, assess the likelihood of success and consider the best use of resources. Three key questions include: Is it in the client's and your best interest? Does the client genuinely want the deal? Is the deal profitable for you? If affirmative, proceed; otherwise, gracefully leave the door open for future opportunities. Avoid letting sunk costs drive excessive investment in an unlikely deal.

Chapter 7 Closing Strategies

The close and the salesperson

Gather a group of business professionals, and the topic of sales closing will spark diverse opinions. Seasoned salespeople may reference strategies from outdated training, while newcomers often express fear of the closing phase. Some argue that closing techniques harm the credibility and trust of salespeople. To address this, we must reevaluate past closing strategies and tackle the perception issue afflicting sales professionals. Stereotypes play a role, with deceptive and aggressive closers contributing to negative perceptions. Movie portrayals, such as Alec Baldwin's "Always be closing" line, further distort the image of salespeople. The use of questionable techniques passed down through generations compounds the problem. The fear of rejection during the close is a legitimate concern, given the effort invested in lead cultivation and objection handling. Proper training and confidence-building are crucial. Common issues in the sales profession include manipulative tactics and the stressful nature of closing. To maintain credibility and trust, it's essential to regularly review and enhance closing strategies, ensuring that the pursuit of a sale doesn't compromise these vital elements.

The buyer and seller relationship

The salesperson's ability to close a deal is intricately tied to demonstrating the value and solution offered by their product or service. Establishing trust is crucial, requiring an understanding of the buyer's challenges and company focus. Building this relationship involves gaining knowledge, addressing objections, and ensuring the buyer feels confident in the promise of delivery. Trust is fostered through thorough preparation for sales calls, honest communication, active listening, and a collaborative approach to developing solutions. Aggressive and manipulative tactics are counterproductive, as successful salespeople prioritize the cornerstones of salesmanship: reputation, credibility, integrity, and character. Recognizing the time needed to cultivate mutual respect and understanding, successful salespeople emphasize the critical importance of the buyer-seller relationship before progressing to the closing stage of the sales process.

The sales process

The actual time spent selling to a customer should be less than 15% of the total time needed to secure the business. The majority of effort is invested in various sales process steps, making it crucial to have a well-designed and strategically aligned process. I advocate for starting with a basic seven to 10-step framework, such as the widely used INP (information, need, product or service) model. Following steps like prospecting, planning, assessing buyer needs, and presenting are crucial. Closing the sale, however, is just the midpoint; success hinges on completing the final four steps, including delivering on promises, following up, and ongoing communication. Reporting and continuous improvement are also vital. Recognizing the importance of each step, successful sales professionals prioritize a finely tuned sales process for successful closings.

The sales presentation

Today is the big day as you prepare to meet your buyer. While the ultimate goal is to close the sale, it's a common mistake for salespeople to rush through the presentation in their eagerness. To avoid this, it's crucial to approach the presentation with a customer-focused strategy and set objectives before attempting to close. Start with a checklist to review details, including product updates, terms, pricing, and delivery schedules. Revisit the customer's requirements, buyer's requests, and your research. Anticipate potential questions or objections, practicing your sales pitch with a balance of confidence and authenticity. Lastly, don't overlook the importance of planning how to utilize the time with your buyer wisely, ensuring ample time for questions, objections, and the closing stage. A well-thought-out strategy is essential for a successful sales presentation and achieving the ultimate objective of closing the sale.

Overcoming obstacles

After prospecting, developing an opportunity, and making a presentation, closing a sale isn't immediate. Handling objections is a crucial part of the process. To navigate this bridge from presentation to closing, anticipate objections related to price, features, or reluctance to change. Practice responses professionally. When confronted, avoid quick responses; it's not a debate. Take a breath, note the objection, and clarify its specifics with follow-up questions. Demonstrate confidence without confrontation, restating positive aspects. This process helps determine if more work is needed or if obstacles are overcome, allowing you to move to the close. Anticipating objections and effectively addressing them is essential for progressing from presentation to closing in the sales process.

Knowing the buyer's signals

A crucial skill for sales success is recognizing the buyer's signals indicating readiness to purchase. Developing expertise in understanding verbal and nonverbal cues is essential for effective communication. Common positive verbal signals include inquiries about pricing, terms, and a request to repeat product features. Visual cues such as eye contact, note-taking, and positive body language are also indicative of readiness. Conversely, signs of distraction, fidgeting, or crossed arms may suggest the need to regroup. Recognizing these signals enhances confidence and signals when it's appropriate to close the sale, making it a vital skill for sales professionals.

Developing your own closing strategy

Becoming a sales professional involves learning various skills, such as pipeline management and presentation methods, often following a company's standardized sales process. However, three topics—prospecting, handling objections, and closing sales—generate diverse opinions and recommendations. While numerous resources offer tips on closing sales, the approach varies, ranging from intense, aggressive tactics to more personalized styles. Developing a closing strategy involves a multi-stage process rooted in trust, active listening, objection handling, belief in the product, and the ability to spot buyer signals for closing. There is no one-size-fits-all formula, and salespeople should continually learn and adapt their strategies throughout their careers.

Ask for the business

After thorough research, planning, and preparation, you've made a successful presentation to a long-sought-after customer. Now, it's time for the crucial closing phase of the sales process. The close involves asking the buyer for a commitment to your offering, typically taking less than a minute. Despite its importance, asking for business is a stressful moment shared by all salespeople. The discomfort stems from asking for commitment, fearing rejection, and the pressure of needing sales for a livelihood. To prepare for the close, there are no magic formulas or shortcuts. Develop personalized closing styles that work for you, believe in yourself, and trust the process. When you sense the right moment, confidently make your close, and embrace the power of silence to let the buyer respond. As a sales professional, the path inevitably leads to the close—ask for the business and seal the deal.

Traditional closing techniques

There are numerous sales closing techniques, with over 100 different strategies available online, each claiming effectiveness. However, it's unnecessary to learn them all. Trust in the buyer-seller relationship is crucial, and closing approaches must consider this trust. Here are four recommended, simple, and honest closing techniques:

1. Summary Close: Recap key features and benefits, briefly restating answers to questions or objections, leading to the question, "Are we ready to move forward?"

2. Balance Sheet Close: Collaboratively discuss pros and cons of the proposal, ensuring confidence in the offering, leading to a positive conclusion statement like, "It feels like we've reached a positive conclusion. Don't you agree?"

3. Needs Close: Focus on providing a solution by checking off items required by the buyer, showcasing the benefits and problem-solving aspects of the offering.

4. Assumptive Close: If based on mutual respect and a strong rapport, it can be used when you know the buyer well enough to say something like, "When should we get started?"

Avoid overthinking the process and choose a closing technique that fits your style, keeping it simple and trust-based for success in sales.

Techniques that push the boundaries

Movies like "Glengarry Glen Ross," "Boiler Room," and "The Wolf of Wall Street" glamorize unethical sales behavior, creating a misleading image of salespeople. Techniques that push ethical boundaries may yield short-term success but damage your reputation and character in the long run. Examples of such techniques include the "Now or Never" close, using scare tactics like the "Negative" close, employing the "Reversal" close to convince the buyer they need something unnecessary, and assuming agreement with the "Assumptive" close. While various closing techniques exist, those involving manipulation, pressure, or gimmicks are outdated and not advisable for maintaining professionalism and long-term client relationships. Always prioritize ethical and professional sales practices.

The sales pipeline

Ultimately, the success of a salesperson is measured by the number of closed sales. To ensure efficiency in the sales process and achieve revenue goals, diligent attention to the sales pipeline is crucial. The sales pipeline visualizes various stages, akin to a funnel, starting with leads and culminating in closed sales. Key performance indicators (KPIs) along the pipeline focus on closed sales and revenue. Three important KPIs include:

1. Sales Leads to Close Ratio: Measures the conversion of leads into closed sales, indicating the effectiveness of lead generation efforts.

2. Sales Win Rate: Determines the success rate of closing opportunities, offering insights into individual sales performance.

3. Deal Size: Evaluates the average volume of closed deals, emphasizing the importance of both closing deals and generating substantial revenue.

Managing the sales pipeline requires constant tracking and optimization of ratios, win rates, and deal sizes to ensure sustained business growth. All sales professionals should be dedicated to refining each stage of the pipeline, from leads to closed sales, to drive revenue growth.

Our job as sales professionals

As a salesperson, emphasize on a straightforward approach to success: focus on solving buyers' needs, be persistent in closing sales, and manage expenses effectively. Simplifying the responsibilities in sales, the ultimate goals are customer satisfaction, revenue generation, and profit maximization. To achieve these objectives, essential steps must be prioritized:

1. Planning and Preparation: This foundational step involves thorough research on customers, competitors, and buyers, anticipating objections, and being ready with clear and honest responses.

2. Know Your Product or Service: Stay informed about product features, benefits, strengths, and weaknesses to address buyer questions effectively and build credibility.

3. Follow a Strategic Sales Process: Progressing strategically through the sales pipeline is crucial. While speeding up the process is ideal, skipping steps risks losing opportunities. Adhering to a well-designed sales process is the best approach.

4. Deliver on Your Promise: Fulfilling commitments made during the sales process is essential for building trust and credibility with buyers, ensuring future collaboration.

5. Communicate and Report Back: Sharing learned skills, such as prospecting, overcoming objections, and closing sales, is vital. Continuous improvement in these responsibilities is key to long-term success.

These responsibilities are critical not only for individual success but also for establishing trust with buyers and achieving sales targets. Mastery of these skills positions a sales professional to provide effective solutions and close more sales throughout their career.

Closing sales in the real world

Closing sales isn't about adopting aggressive stereotypes seen in movies or forceful tactics. In the real world, it involves following your sales process, meticulous planning, and building trust with your buyer to address their needs. With each person having a unique style, there's no fixed roadmap to closing deals; rather, it's about developing a personalized strategy. Learn from fellow professionals, seek feedback, and continuously improve. Listen to your buyer, have confidence in your product, and recognize the signals indicating their readiness to buy. When the time is right, ask for the business and close the sale.

Chapter 8 Using AI and Automation to Sell More

Exploring areas of automation and AI in sales

To explore the benefits of AI and automation in sales, we must first identify tasks that could be automated. Tasks fall into three main categories: prospecting, selling, and post-sales/administration. Prospecting involves finding and reaching prospective customers, including searching for targets, gathering insights, and scheduling meetings. Selling includes building proposals, managing the pipeline, closing deals, fulfilling orders, and invoicing. Post-sales/administration involves customer care, additional sales, forecasting, and reporting. These activities are time-consuming and prone to human error. AI and automation tools can enhance efficiency and accuracy in prospecting and other sales tasks.

Sales prospecting with AI and automation tools

Prospecting is a crucial but time-consuming aspect of sales, involving identifying and reaching out to potential customers. Often referred to as lead generation, it encompasses cold, warm, and inbound leads, forming the foundation for building relationships and creating opportunities. While skills like pipeline management and sales presentations are important, they are ineffective without successful prospecting. Automation and AI tools can significantly aid in this process by expediting tasks, handling repetitive actions, and analyzing data for valuable insights. AI and automation benefit sales prospecting in lead enrichment, optimizing communication through emails and direct messages, efficient meeting scheduling, and gaining insights from marketing activities.

Lead enrichment with AI and automation

Lead enrichment expedites the qualification process by adding extra details to a lead record. This includes essential information such as the lead's name, company, and position, as well as more insightful data like social channels, past interactions, and in-depth company details. In the past, obtaining this information was time-consuming, requiring manual searches. Automation streamlines this process, providing real-time updates without repeated efforts. AI enhances the value by identifying the vendors and solutions currently used by prospects. This knowledge offers insights into their current spending, preferences, and potential areas for future investment. AI can analyze data, reveal opportunities, identify white space, and provide models for understanding prospects' needs and challenges. Integrated with CRM, these tools offer quick access to comprehensive information, resembling the guidance of an experienced sector-specific salesperson, instantly available at the click of a button.

Emailing and direct messages

Email automation is a widely utilized tool in marketing for reaching large audiences efficiently. While traditional Mail Merge has been around since the eighties, modern email automation goes beyond simple personalization. It's crucial to avoid errors in personalization, as addressing prospects incorrectly can harm relationships. AI and automation have evolved from the Mail Merge era, introducing features like sequencing, allowing the creation of automated journeys with intelligence—pausing sequences upon prospect replies to prevent awkward moments. A/B testing with different templates and integrating APIs for data retrieval are additional capabilities. The most notable advancement is AI's ability to analyze vast amounts of data on successful and unsuccessful emails, considering factors like word count, language, questions asked, formatting, emojis, and more. AI can assess and suggest improvements to enhance email effectiveness, resulting in increased response rates with minimal adjustments.

Meeting scheduling for sales professionals

Booking time with prospects, whether for cold, warm, or inbound leads, is highly valuable for relationship building and presenting solutions. However, it's challenging due to busy schedules. The key is demonstrating the value of the meeting and minimizing the prospect's time and effort as the cost. Automation and AI tools can assist in reducing the effort needed to schedule a meeting. By emphasizing the gains (insights and solutions) and minimizing the cost (time and effort), prospects are more likely to agree. Utilizing tools that link with calendars and display availability simplifies the scheduling process. One effective tool shares a link for prospects to choose a suitable time, automatically updating calendars and reducing the back-and-forth communication. This approach not only minimizes the prospect's time and effort but also streamlines the scheduling process, making it efficient and stress-free.

Gathering insights from marketing

Salespeople desire comprehensive information about prospects and their activities, including website visits, preferences, roles within companies, and buying history. Data protection laws restrict access to detailed information, but some software providers push boundaries within legal limits, offering valuable insights. Traditional marketing metrics, such as website views and search engine rankings, provide general information. However, advanced tools can offer more specific insights by tracking IP addresses and connecting with CRM data. For instance, if targeting a head of recruitment, the tool can identify a company's IP address and extract related CRM details, saving time and increasing the likelihood of engaging with interested prospects. While the tools cannot identify individual visitors due to privacy laws, they provide valuable information for targeted outreach and generic insights, enabling sales teams to make informed calls to potentially interested companies.

The process of selling

After capturing the prospect's attention and identifying opportunities, the selling phase is where salespeople truly demonstrate their value. This crucial stage involves managing the pipeline, creating quotes and proposals, closing deals, and handling invoicing and payments. While there are additional tasks like presenting solutions and overcoming objections. We'll explore available tools, advantages, and potential pitfalls in each of these tasks.

Managing sales deals with AI and automation

Deal management involves overseeing all open and active opportunities, akin to the challenge of spinning plates in a circus act. The goal is to prevent opportunities from losing momentum and being lost. Like performers monitoring spinning plates, salespeople must identify slowing opportunities and provide momentum to prevent them from falling. While setting manual reminders in calendars is a basic approach, CRM systems offer tools to automate this process. Some systems notify when a deal needs attention, reset timers upon customer interaction, and track key dates like contract renewals. Emphasizing the importance of using such tools, the advice is not to attempt to be a circus performer but to leverage technology for easier and more efficient deal management. Check your active opportunities and reach out to those that haven't been contacted in a while.

Building proposals with AI and automation

Creating a proposal is a critical juncture in the sales process, and AI offers significant assistance beyond basic CRM capabilities. Basic CRM systems can streamline the process by pulling product information directly from a database, minimizing errors, and saving time. Advanced AI tools excel in handling Requests for Proposal (RFPs), reading and interpreting massive documents, extracting relevant sections and questions, and even suggesting responses from a content library. This dramatically reduces the time spent on RFP responses, alleviating stress and allowing salespeople to focus on relationship-building and pursuing more opportunities.

AI also enhances the customer's experience by enabling the creation of fully online proposals shared as links, rather than traditional documents or locked PDFs. Within the online platform, prospects can interact with the proposal, selecting options and exploring various combinations of products. The tool, equipped with live pricing calculators, keeps the total updated in real-time, allowing prospects to see how changes impact the final price. While relinquishing some control to the software and the prospect, the salesperson maintains control over the initial proposal content. This sharing of power can strengthen the client relationship, provided it is executed thoughtfully, aligning with the prospect's requirements and making business sense for the salesperson.

Completing sales deals with AI and automation

In the crucial deal completion stage, swift action is essential to prevent potential obstacles from derailing the agreement. Delays can lead to changing needs, budget constraints, competitor interference, or waning interest. AI and automation, while not capable of closing deals, excel at removing obstacles. Digital contracts, facilitated by accessible software, enable online collaboration, real-time updates, and electronic signatures. Linked to CRM systems, signed contracts trigger notifications, allowing prompt order processing and automatic filing. This approach saves time, money, and environmental resources compared to traditional physical contract signing methods. Additionally, salespeople benefit from templates, drag-and-drop tools, and CRM integration, streamlining the contract creation process and maintaining momentum in the sales opportunity. Automate the contract signing process for efficiency.

Invoicing in your sales process using AI and automation

Having completed the sales process, including relationship building, understanding needs, presenting value propositions, overcoming objections, and closing the deal, the final step is to secure the agreed-upon payment. However, salespeople, focused on maintaining relationships and closing deals, often lack the time and bandwidth to pursue payment collection. AI and automation offer solutions, starting with automatic invoice generation using CRM and accounting systems. Templates or software can pull information from databases, speeding up the process and reducing errors. Additionally, AI-powered accountancy tools can automate the task of chasing payments by tracking payment terms and sending reminders to both the salesperson and the customer. Some tools even provide online payment portals, streamlining the payment process for customers and avoiding awkward conversations about payment collection, allowing salespeople to concentrate on relationship development.

How post-sales and forecasting may be automated

While finding and closing prospects is a primary focus, the work doesn't end there. Salespeople must strategize and forecast their approach to meet targets and ensure customer satisfaction through follow-ups and additional sales. Sales leaders need to monitor team performance, provide training, and receive sales forecasts. However, time is a luxury salespeople lack. AI and automation can alleviate this burden by speeding up tasks like forecasting, traditionally challenging for sales professionals. AI helps make sense of the pipeline by combining human factors like relationships and trust with statistical data, resulting in accurate and quantifiable predictions. AI and automation tools enhance effectiveness beyond the sales process.

Strategy and forecasting in sales

Aside from desiring increased sales, predicting the future remains impossible, advancements in AI, automation, and machine learning enable increasingly precise sales predictions. Computers rapidly analyze vast amounts of historical data to offer projections, considering factors like time of year, past performance, and updated pricing. Salespeople can also predict individual performance by assigning probabilities to deal stages. Automation systems use this data, compare it to active details and close dates, and provide a predicted revenue within a specified timeframe, serving as a gauge rather than a guaranteed outcome. Additionally, AI contributes to forecasting through data visualization tools, converting complex data into easily understandable dashboards. These tools help sales professionals comprehend their progress against targets, identify major opportunities, save time on data presentation, and equip managers with the necessary insights for business preparation.

Improving customer support efficiency

After winning a client and securing our commission, customer retention becomes crucial. Customer support is paramount for existing clients, ranging from simple inquiries to urgent problem resolution. However, as we focus on expanding our customer base, AI can alleviate the workload associated with customer service. AI systems excel at time-saving and efficiency in handling repetitive tasks. In customer service, AI aids in categorizing incoming requests, such as sorting urgent emails based on tonality or deadlines. It can respond automatically to simple queries or flag complex ones for manual handling. In ticketing situations, AI analyzes customer submissions, automatically categorizing them by urgency or required skill. However, caution is advised, as AI can make mistakes if not properly configured and monitored. It's crucial to use AI wisely, considering factors like response time and potential errors, while evaluating time savings and bottlenecks in the customer request process.

Using automation tools to sell small items

After completing a sale, customers often return for small additional items, like cables or accessories. While these transactions may seem less lucrative due to low commissions, customer retention is vital. However, handling these small purchases doesn't require AI; instead, automation proves useful. Integration between websites and CRMs allows for a simple portal where customers can order small items directly, displaying all necessary information. This benefits both parties, as customers can swiftly make purchases without upselling discussions, and salespeople can stay focused on larger opportunities. Nevertheless, maintaining a personal touch by occasionally expressing gratitude to customers for their purchases enhances the relationship aspect of sales.

Using automation tools to gather sales statistics

Monitoring a salesperson's performance is valuable for assessing activity levels and providing insights for training. Increased activity often correlates with more opportunities and sales. However, it's essential to analyze detailed metrics to identify specific areas of improvement. AI can assist by recording and analyzing various metrics like call success rates, meeting conversions, and more. Advanced CRM systems can even assess conversational flow, tone, talk time, and prospect emotion during calls. This enables targeted training based on individual or team needs, offering valuable insights into performance without the need for time-consuming manual monitoring.

Continuing to grow your sales AI and automation mindset

Using AI and automation tools has both benefits and drawbacks. While they save time, reduce errors, and provide valuable insights, there's a risk of damaging relationships with impersonal interactions. The decision to employ these tools becomes simpler as their advantages increasingly outweigh the disadvantages. With evolving functionality, there are more opportunities to delegate tasks to AI. It's crucial to choose tools wisely, regularly assess options, and evaluate the value they bring to your business.

Automation and AI Software Recommendations:

1. Sales Prospecting and Lead Generation:

   - Lead Enrichment: HubSpot (www.hubspot.com)

   - Lead Enrichment: ZoomInfo (zoominfo.com/solutions/sales)

   - SalesOS (www.salesos.io)

2. Email Sequencing:

   - HubSpot (www.hubspot.com)

   - Reply.io AI Email Assistant (get.reply.io/download)

3. Judging Emails and Messages:

   - Reply.io AI Email Assistant (get.reply.io/download)

4. Meeting Scheduling:

   - Calendly (calendly.com/solutions/sales)

5. Gathering Insights from Marketing:

   - LeadFeeder (Compatible with: HubSpot) (leadfeeder.grsm.io/download)

6. Selling Processes:

   - Managing Sales Opportunities: HubSpot (www.hubspot.com)

   - Building Proposals: RFPIO (rfpio.com)

   - Completing Sales Deals: DocuSign (www.docusign.com)

7. Invoicing:

- HubSpot (www.hubspot.com)

8. Post Sales and Forecasting:

  - Strategy and Forecasting: Databox (Compatible with: HubSpot) (databox.com)

9. Customer and Support Efficiency:

  - Levity (levity.ai/)

10. Selling Small Items:

  - HubSpot (www.hubspot.com)

11. Gathering Sales Statistics:

  - Pickle AI (pickleai.com/)